HISTORY CORNER

popcorn

The Gunpowder Plot

Jenny Powell

Explore the world with **Popcorn** - your complete first non-fiction library.

Look out for more titles in the **Popcorn** range. All books have the same format of simple text and striking images. Text is carefully matched to the pictures to help readers to identify and understand key vocabulary.
www.waylandbooks.co.uk/popcorn

First published in 2009 by Wayland
Reprinted in 2010 by Wayland

This paperback edition published in 2011 by Wayland

Wayland
Hachette Children's Books
338 Euston Road
London NW1 3BH

Wayland Australia
Level 17/207 Kent Street
Sydney NSW 2000

Editor: Katie Powell
Designer: Phipps Design

British Library Cataloguing in Publication Data
Powell, Jenny
Gunpowder Plot. - (Popcorn. History corner)
1. Fawkes, Guy, 1570-1606 - Juvenile literature
2. Gunpowder Plot, 1605 - Juvenile literature
3. Great Britain - History - James I, 1603-1625 - Juvenile literature
I. Title
941'.061

ISBN: 978 0 7502 6685 7

Printed and bound in China

Wayland is a division of Hachette Children's Books, an Hachette UK company.
www.hachette.co.uk

Photographs:
Mary Evans Picture Library/Alamy: titlepage, 4, 14, 18, Tim Gander/Alamy: 20, Hulton Archive/Getty Images: 2, 8, 10, 16, 17, 19, The London Art Archive/Alamy: 6, 13, Popperfoto/Getty Images: 9, The Print Collector/Alamy: 15, Private Collection/Archives Charmet/Bridgeman Art Library, London: 11, Steve Sant/Alamy: 7, Alex Segre/Alamy: 5, StockyStock/Alamy: 21
Cover: Carlo Molinari

Contents

What was the Gunpowder Plot? 4

Catholics and Protestants 6

A plot is formed 8

Guy Fawkes 10

How did they do it? 12

The plot is leaked 14

Guy Fawkes is captured 16

Torture and confession 18

Celebrations then and now 20

Timeline 22

Make a 'Wanted' poster 23

Glossary 24

Index 24

What was the Gunpowder Plot?

On the 5th of November 1605, some men plotted to blow up the Houses of Parliament. They wanted to kill James I, the king of England.

The gunpowder plotters' plan was called the Gunpowder Plot.

The Houses of Parliament are important buildings where Britain's laws are made.

This is a picture of the Houses of Parliament today.

Catholics and Protestants

In 1605, some people in England were Catholics and some were Protestants. King James I was a Protestant. He passed laws to make everyone become Protestant.

King James I was the king of England for 22 years.

Catholics were forced to worship in secret. They were fined or put in prison if they did not go to a Protestant church service on Sundays.

You can see the hole in the floor where a Catholic priest would have hidden.

A plot is formed

A Catholic man called Robert Catesby met with a group of other men. They made a plot to kill King James I.

Robert Catesby's father refused to become a Protestant. He spent most of his life in prison.

Robert Catesby was the leader of the plot.

The men decided to blow up the Houses of Parliament when the king was inside.

The men met in secret to talk about the plot.

Guy Fawkes

The plotters had heard about a Catholic man named Guy Fawkes. He had been a soldier in the Spanish army and knew how to use gunpowder.

This is a drawing of Guy Fawkes.

Guy Fawkes wanted to be allowed to be Catholic so he agreed to be involved in the plot.

Guy Fawkes fought in the Spanish army because Spain was a Catholic country.

How did they do it?

The plotters rented a cellar underneath the Houses of Parliament. They hid 36 barrels of gunpowder there.

Guy Fawkes' job was to guard the gunpowder.

The men chose 5th November 1605 as the day of the explosion. They knew the king was going to be at Parliament that day.

Can you see the plotters in the cellar underneath Parliament?

The plot is leaked

A Catholic minister called Lord Monteagle received a letter warning him not to attend the opening of Parliament on 5th November.

We will probably never know who wrote this secret letter.

my lord out of the love i beare you to some of youere frends
i have a caer of youer preservacion therfor i would
advyse yowe as yowe tender youer lyf to devys some
excuse to shift of youer attendance at this parleament
for god and man hath concurred to punishe the wickednes
of this tyme and thinke not slightlye of this advertisment
but retyere youre self into youre contri wheare yowe
maye expect the event in safti for thowghe theare be no
apparance of anni stir yet i saye they shall receyve a terrible
blowe this parleament and yet they shall not seie who
hurts them this councel is not to be contemned because
it maye do yowe good and can do yowe no harme for the
dangere is passed as soon as yowe have burnt the letter
and i hope god will give yowe the grace to mak good
use of it to whose holy proteccion i comend yowe

To the right honorable
the lord monteagle

Lord Monteagle decided to show the letter to the king. News of the secret plot had leaked out!

As a reward for warning the king, Lord Monteagle was given lots of land and money.

After Lord Monteagle had read the letter he went straight to the king.

Guy Fawkes is captured

On 5th November, King James I ordered a search of the Houses of Parliament. His men found Guy Fawkes and the hidden gunpowder.

The king's men searched the cellars underneath the Houses of Parliament.

Guy Fawkes was arrested and taken to the Tower of London. The other plotters went into hiding.

King James I wanted to meet the man who had plotted to kill him.

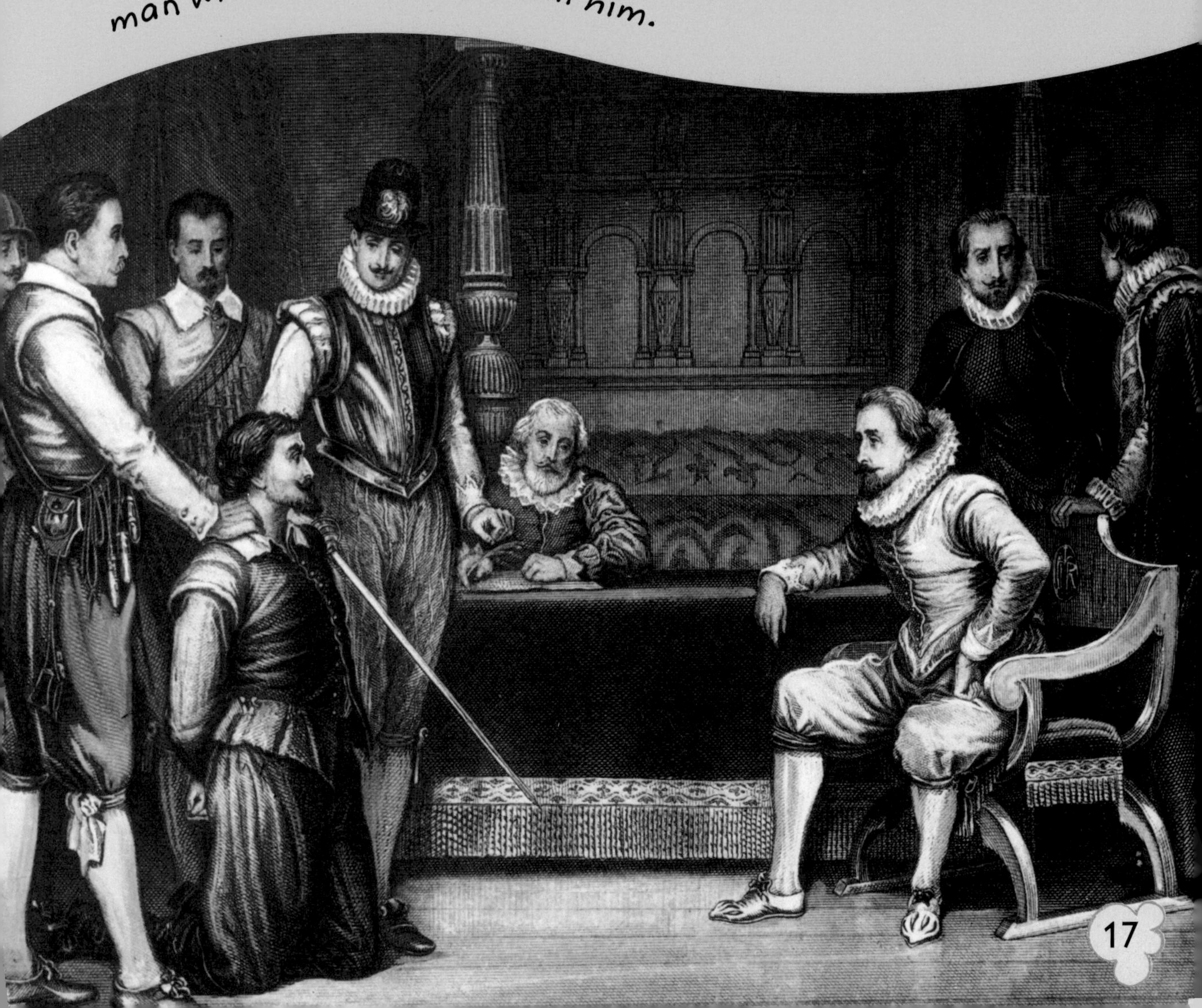

Torture and confession

Guy Fawkes was tortured into naming the other members of the Gunpowder Plot. All the plotters were soon killed or captured.

Guy Fawkes confessed to being involved in the plot.

The men went to court where they were found guilty of treason. They were sentenced to death.

Guy Fawkes signed two confessions. His second signature is harder to read because he had been tortured.

Guy Fawkes' first signature

Guy Fawkes' second signature

Celebrations then and now

That night, bonfires were lit to celebrate the king's survival.

Today, we still light bonfires on 5th November.

Every year, Bonfire night on 5th November reminds us all of the failed Gunpowder Plot.

A figure of Guy Fawkes is often put on top of the bonfire.

Timeline

1570	Guy Fawkes is born.
1573	Robert Catesby, the leader of the Gunpowder Plot, is born.
1593	Guy Fawkes joins the Spanish army.
1603	**24th March**, Queen Elizabeth I of England dies. King James VI of Scotland becomes James I of England.
1605	The plotters rent a cellar under the Houses of Parliament and hide 36 barrels of gunpowder there.
1605	**26th October**, Lord Monteagle receives a letter, warning him not to go to Parliament on 5th November.
1605	**5th November**, King James I orders a search of the Houses of Parliament and Guy Fawkes is arrested.
1605	**7th November**, Guy Fawkes confesses to the plot.
1605	Some of the plotters, including Robert Catesby, are shot dead at Holbeach House in Worcestershire. The rest are captured.
1606	The plotters are tried for treason in court and are found guilty.
1606	**31st January**, Guy Fawkes and other members of the Gunpowder Plot are killed for treason.

Make a 'Wanted' poster

You will need:

- 1 piece of A4 white card
- some charcoal

Have fun making your own 'Wanted' poster by following these simple instructions.

1. Use the edge of the charcoal to lightly colour in the background of the paper.

2. Use the tip of the charcoal to draw Guy Fawkes in the middle of the page. You will need to press quite hard.

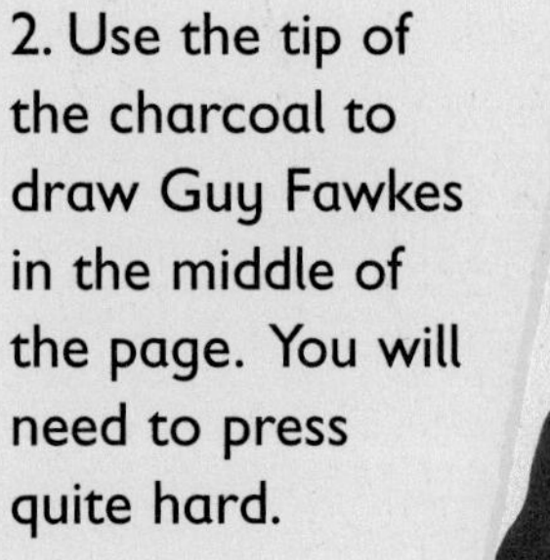

3. Draw a hat on Guy Fawkes (think about the sort of hat he would have worn in 1605).

4. Add a 'Wanted' title at the top of the page in big letters.

5. Then add a reward amount onto your poster.

Glossary

arrested
when someone is stopped by the police

Catholics
people who believe that the Pope is the head of the Catholic church

cellar
a room underground

confess
when someone admits to a crime

fined
to pay money for doing something wrong

gunpowder
a powder that easily explodes when it is set alight

Protestants
people who believe that the king or queen is the head of the Church of England

rented
to pay for the use of a room

torture
when someone is hurt or punished

treason
a crime against the country or its king or queen

worship
when someone prays to God

Index

bonfire 20, 21

Catesby, Robert 8, 22
Catholic 6-7, 8, 10, 11, 14
cellar 12, 13, 16, 22
church 7

Elizabeth I, Queen 22

Fawkes, Guy 10-11, 16, 17, 18, 22

gunpowder 10, 12, 16, 22

Houses of Parliament 4, 5, 9, 12, 16, 22

James I, King 4, 6, 8, 9, 13, 15, 16, 17, 20, 22

law 5, 6
letter 14, 15, 22

Monteagle, Lord 14, 15, 22

Protestant 6-7, 8

Spanish army 10, 11

Tower of London 17
treason 19

worship 7